Linking art to the world around us

artyfacts

Structures and Materials

FRONT COVER IMAGES: DAVID TOMLINSON/ BRUCE COLEMAN COLLECTION; D & J HEATON/ SPECTRUM COLOUR LIBRARY; JEREMY HORNER/ CORBIS

CONCEPT

Publisher: Felicia L[...]

Design: Tracy Carrington

Editorial Planning: Karen Foster

Research and Development: Gerry Bailey, Alec Edgington

PROJECT DEVELOPMENT

Project Director: Karen Foster

Editors: Claire Sipi, Hazel Songhurst, Samantha Sweeney

Design Director: Tracy Carrington

Design Manager: Flora Awolaja

Design and DTP: Claire Penny, Paul Montague, James Thompson, Mark Dempsey

Photo and Art Editor: Andrea Sadler

Illustrator: Jan Smith

Model Artist: Sophie Dean

Further models: Sue Partington, Abigail Dean

Digital Workflow: Edward MacDermott

Production: Victoria Grimsell, Christina Brown

Scanning: Acumen Colour Ltd

Published by Abbey Children's Books
(a division of Abbey Home Media Group)

Abbey Home Media Group
435-437 Edgware Road
London W2 1TH
United Kingdom

Printed and bound by Dai Nippon, Hong Kong

Linking art to the world around us

artyfacts
Structures
and Materials

Contents

WRITTEN BY Barbara Taylor

Stained glass

The glass of a window pane is hard, flat and transparent. Amazingly, it is made from a mix of ingredients that you could find on a beach. Glass is made from sand, quartz, potash and lime. When these are heated together and then cooled, they make glass.

COLOURS FROM METALS

People have been making glass in this way for centuries. The ingredients are heated in large vats, where they become transparent, liquid glass. The liquid is either left clear, or it can be 'stained' by adding ground metals or other chemicals. The metal cobalt gives glass a brilliant blue colour. Red glass is made using the metals gold, copper or selenium. Green glass can be made using the metal chromium.

PICTURES IN GLASS

Coloured glass is often used in windows. These windows are usually made by skilled artists. The artist must cut the pieces of coloured glass and arrange them in a picture or pattern. The glass pieces are then welded together using molten lead strips. Perhaps the most beautiful coloured glass of all is to be seen in the stained glass windows of churches and cathedrals.

When the sunlight shines through this stained glass window, pools of coloured light fill the room.

Materials

Sun-catcher

black card

light-coloured pencil

scissors

tape

coloured tissue paper

glue

1 Mark out a pattern of shapes on a piece of black card.

2 Cut out the shapes, leaving a frame around each.

3 Glue scraps of coloured tissue paper behind the spaces in each frame.

Make up your own colourful window designs

4 Tape your pattern onto a window so that the light shines through.

For a neater finish, cut out with a craft knife – but ask an adult to help you or do it for you.

5

Warm wax

When we want light we just flick a switch. But before electricity, wax candles were the main light source for most people. They were used in ancient Egypt as long as 5,000 years ago where they were even used to tell the time. A scale marked on the side of a candle clock showed how much it would burn down in an hour.

FLAMES OF GAS

A candle is a long cylinder of wax with a piece of string running through it. The end of the string – the wick – sticks out of the top of the candle. As the candle burns, heat from the flame melts the wax at the base of the wick. The heat causes the liquid wax to flow up the wick and turns into a gas.

FLOWERS AND SEALS

Worker bees make wax to build the walls of the six-sided cells in their honeycomb. The wax comes from special glands under their abdomens. We collect it by removing the honey, melting the comb, straining off impurities and then pouring the pure wax into molds until it sets. We use the beeswax as a modelling material and to make candles. It is also used in furniture and floor waxes, waxed paper and ointments. In the past, wax was used for seals – stamps fixed to a letter or document. The wax was held over the paper and melted with a candle. A design was then pressed into the soft drops of wax. As the wax cooled, it set hard, holding the envelope or sheets of paper together. The seal could only be broken by the person the letter was addressed to.

Materials

WHAT YOU NEED

large candle

sequins

darning needle

glue

glitter

brush

paints

Carved candle

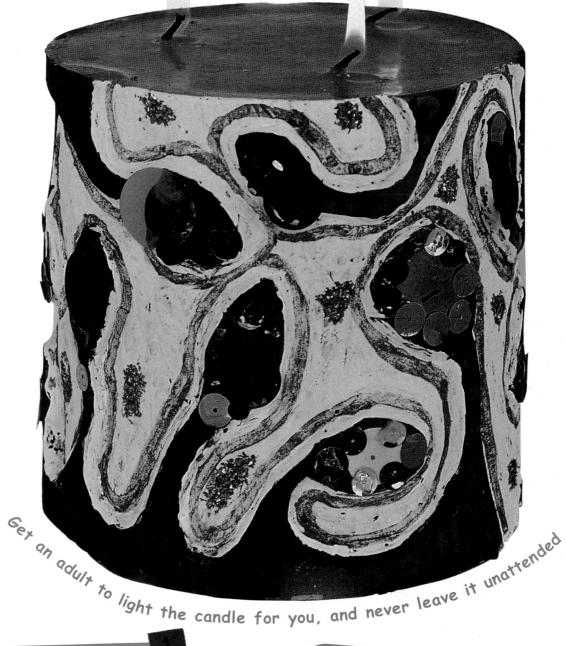

Get an adult to light the candle for you, and never leave it unattended

1 Carve a pattern on the candle with the darning kneedle or any other carving tool.

Paint the candle, and decorate the carved areas with sequins and glitter. **2**

7

Pictures on walls

In some parts of the world, huge, colourful pictures decorate the outside walls of buildings. In India and Egypt, paintings of gods, people and animals make some streets look like giant picture books. Many old houses in Germany and Switzerland are painted with pictures from religious stories or folk tales.

CAVE PAINTINGS

Thousands of years ago, people in Europe, Africa and Australia painted pictures on the walls of caves. The pictures showed animals and hunters. They were the first wall paintings, called murals. The caves may have been temples for celebrating successful hunting trips. The paintings may also have been used to make magic to help the hunters on their trips.

MODERN MURALS

People still paint pictures on walls. The pictures might be painted to brighten up a neighbourhood, a playground or a building. Colourful pictures of suns, trees, flowers, animals and people can change a dull, ugly wall into a bright, interesting place.

GRAFFITI ART

Rough drawings, writing or marks on the walls of buildings is called graffiti. But scribbling on walls is nothing new. Ancient graffiti was found scrawled on the walls of Egyptian tombs and pyramids, Greek temples and Roman buildings. Today, in cities such as New York, well-known graffiti artists cover the walls of public places with colourful art.

Frieze art

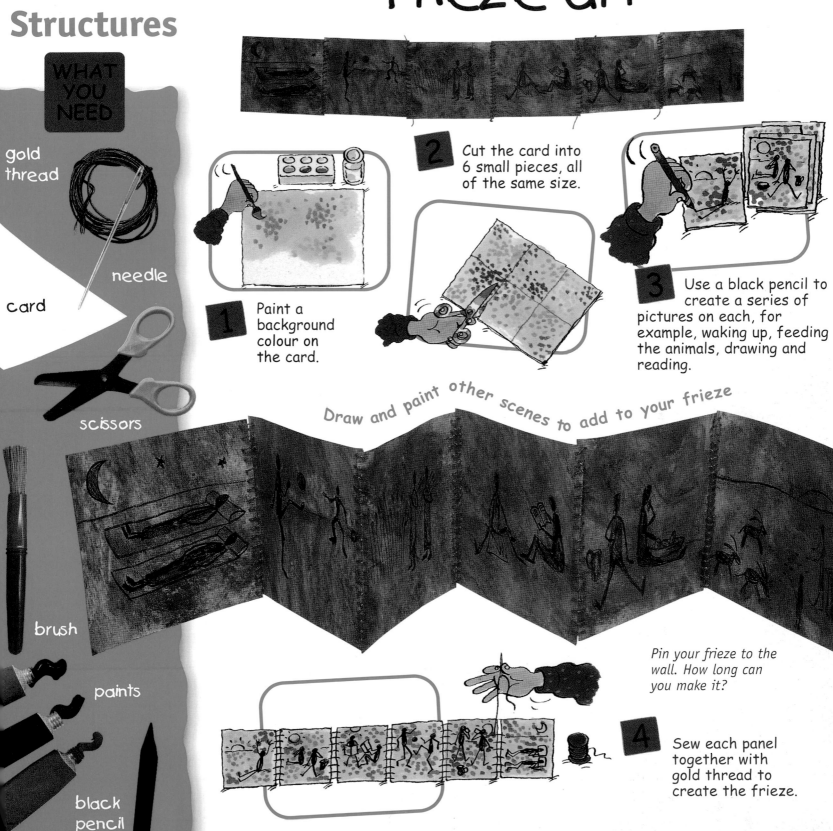

WHAT YOU NEED

gold thread

needle

card

scissors

brush

paints

black pencil

1 Paint a background colour on the card.

2 Cut the card into 6 small pieces, all of the same size.

3 Use a black pencil to create a series of pictures on each, for example, waking up, feeding the animals, drawing and reading.

Draw and paint other scenes to add to your frieze

Pin your frieze to the wall. How long can you make it?

4 Sew each panel together with gold thread to create the frieze.

9

Tents and teepees

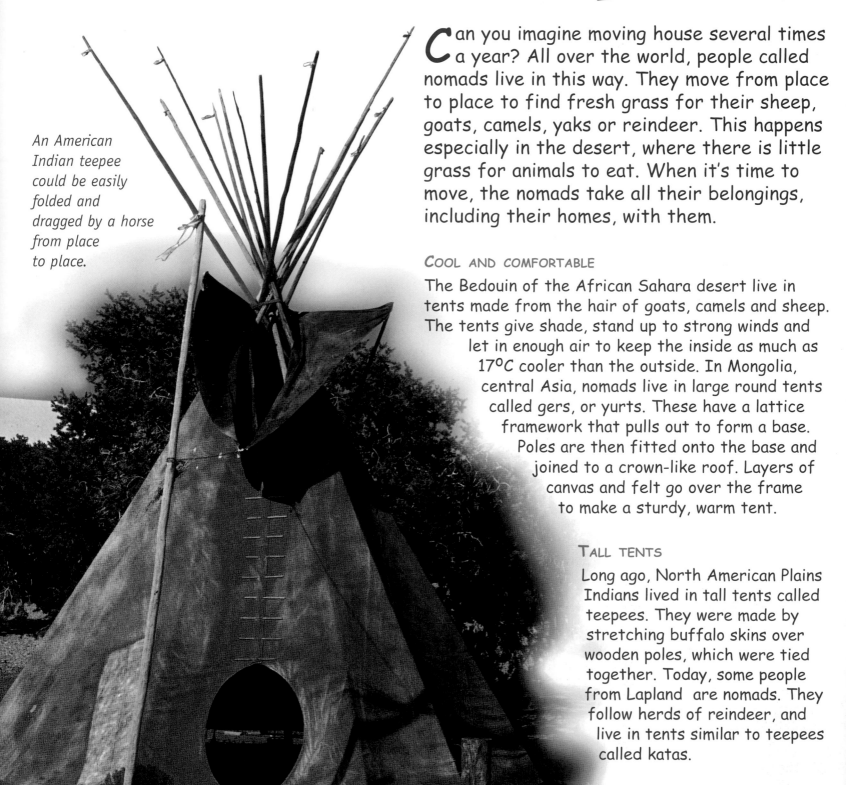

An American Indian teepee could be easily folded and dragged by a horse from place to place.

*C*an you imagine moving house several times a year? All over the world, people called nomads live in this way. They move from place to place to find fresh grass for their sheep, goats, camels, yaks or reindeer. This happens especially in the desert, where there is little grass for animals to eat. When it's time to move, the nomads take all their belongings, including their homes, with them.

COOL AND COMFORTABLE

The Bedouin of the African Sahara desert live in tents made from the hair of goats, camels and sheep. The tents give shade, stand up to strong winds and let in enough air to keep the inside as much as 17ºC cooler than the outside. In Mongolia, central Asia, nomads live in large round tents called gers, or yurts. These have a lattice framework that pulls out to form a base. Poles are then fitted onto the base and joined to a crown-like roof. Layers of canvas and felt go over the frame to make a sturdy, warm tent.

TALL TENTS

Long ago, North American Plains Indians lived in tall tents called teepees. They were made by stretching buffalo skins over wooden poles, which were tied together. Today, some people from Lapland are nomads. They follow herds of reindeer, and live in tents similar to teepees called katas.

Native American camp

Structures

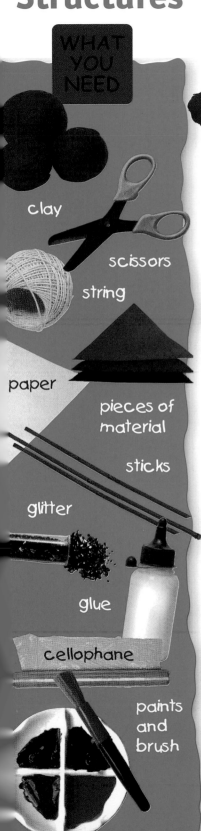

WHAT YOU NEED

clay

scissors

string

paper

pieces of material

sticks

glitter

glue

cellophane

paints and brush

1 Cut out semicircles of material and paint patterns onto them.

2 Tie together 5 sticks and wrap a semicircle of material around them. Glue into place.

3 To make the fire, scrunch up strips of paper into balls. Paint and glue them on a circular piece of card as shown above.

4 Glue flame-shaped pieces of cellophane into the centre of the card. Sprinkle on glitter.

6 Make people for your teepees. Use clay to make their heads and feet, string for their hair and sticks for their bodies. Use scraps of material for their clothes.

5 Paint small rolls of paper brown to make logs, and place the fire in the middle of your teepee.

Make and decorate other teepees for your camp

11

House of sticks

For thousands of years, people all around the world have lived in longhouses. A longhouse is a large house made from wood. It is usually big enough for a whole tribe to live in all together. In Borneo, a traditional longhouse may be as long as a street! As many as fifty families may live, cook, eat and sleep inside.

BUILDING A LONGHOUSE

A longhouse is built using a row of wooden columns to hold up a central roof pole. Matching rows of columns mark the walls on each side. The roof pole is joined to the wall beams by lengths of wood called rafters. The roof is covered with bundles of dried grasses or reeds.

The walls may be made of clay, or thatched with grasses or reeds. In the past, American woodland Indians used tree bark and Europeans used woven twigs plastered with clay.

STILTS AND DOME STRUCTURES

In Indonesia and Polynesia, longhouses are raised above the ground on stilts to protect them from the floods in the rainy season. Each family has its own sleeping area and place to work. The rest of the house is one enormous room, which everyone shares and uses for eating, music and dancing. Until the 19th century, the Iroquois Indians of the north-eastern United States lived in wood-and-bark longhouses. Their domed roofs were made by bending thin trees from posts on one side over to the other side. This frame was then covered in bark. Cooking was done in the middle of the house, where an opening in the roof acted as a chimney.

Structures

WHAT YOU NEED

cardboard box

card

scissors

hay

string

lolly sticks

cocktail sticks

glue

beach mat

corrugated card

1 Cut window shapes and a door in the box. Cover the box, apart from the flaps, with lolly sticks.

2 Gather bunches of hay and tie each end with string. Stick them onto a length of card and then glue the card onto the front flap of the box.

3 Make stilts by rolling up pieces of corrugated card. Stick them to the bottom of the house. Glue lolly sticks onto the stilts, as shown.

4 Glue lolly sticks onto a length of card to make a verandah. Make a ladder from cocktail sticks and string.

5 Cut a rectangle and two triangular shapes from a beachmat, to make the sides and back of the roof. Glue them to the house and then glue the front roof, on a slant, to them.

Make cardboard cut-out people for your hut

13

Bricks and mortar

People have been using bricks to build with for thousands of years. Six thousand years ago, the Egyptians made bricks from mud mixed with straw. They left them in the sun to harden, or baked them in a type of oven called a kiln. Even today in hot countries, some people still use this method of making mud bricks to build their homes.

DESIGNED FOR STRENGTH

Today, buildings can be made from many different materials. Some are constructed from steel, glass, plastic or some other high-tech material. But many continue to be built with bricks and mortar using traditional methods.

BRICKLAYING

Look closely at a brick wall to see how the bricks are arranged: they are placed in an overlapping pattern. Arranging the bricks like this gives the wall more strength. To increase the strength, the bricks are then stuck together with a layer of mortar. This is usually made by mixing together cement, lime, sand and water.

ROUGH OR SMOOTH

Bricks can be made with many different surface textures, ranging from smooth to rough. They also come in different colours, depending on the colour of the material they are made from.

BUILDERS' TOOLS

Building brick walls is a skilled job. The walls need to be straight, otherwise the building will be unsafe and might topple over. Builders use special tools to help them construct the walls of buildings properly. A plumb line – a heavy weight on a string – is used to make sure the walls are vertical. A spirit level is used to make sure the rows of bricks are horizontal. The bricklayer stacks the bricks in an open wooden box attached to a pole, called a hod, to carry them on a building site. A trowel is used to spread the mortar that cements the bricks together. It is also used to tap the bricks firmly in place.

A courtyard entrance, built using traditional methods.

Building collage

Materials

WHAT YOU NEED

scissors

crayons

mounting card

coloured paper

glue

pencil

1 Using crayons and paper, take rubbings of different surfaces inside and outside your home.

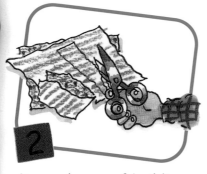

2 Draw shapes of buildings onto your rubbings and cut them out.

3 Glue the shapes onto the mounting card to form a row of different buildings.

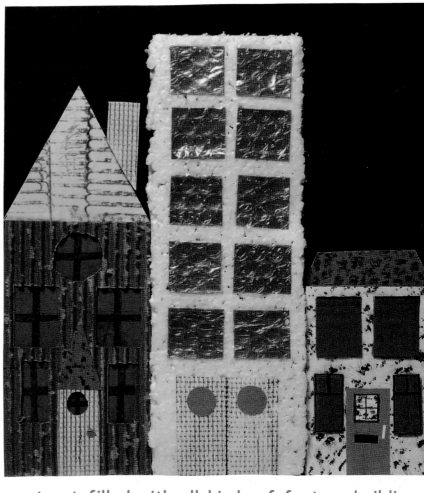

Invent a street filled with all kinds of fantasy buildings!

15

Cities on water

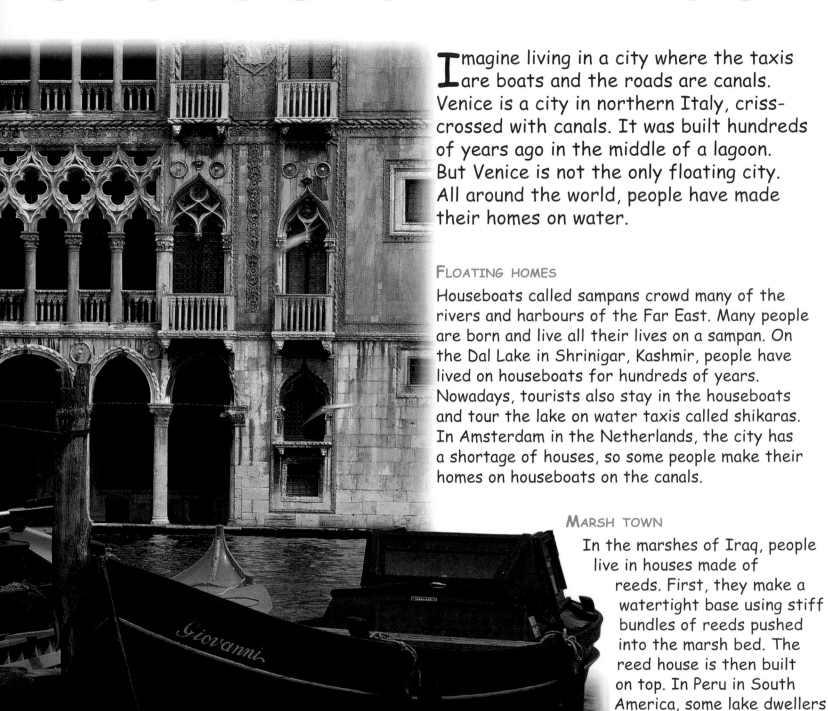

Imagine living in a city where the taxis are boats and the roads are canals. Venice is a city in northern Italy, criss-crossed with canals. It was built hundreds of years ago in the middle of a lagoon. But Venice is not the only floating city. All around the world, people have made their homes on water.

FLOATING HOMES

Houseboats called sampans crowd many of the rivers and harbours of the Far East. Many people are born and live all their lives on a sampan. On the Dal Lake in Shrinigar, Kashmir, people have lived on houseboats for hundreds of years. Nowadays, tourists also stay in the houseboats and tour the lake on water taxis called shikaras. In Amsterdam in the Netherlands, the city has a shortage of houses, so some people make their homes on houseboats on the canals.

MARSH TOWN

In the marshes of Iraq, people live in houses made of reeds. First, they make a watertight base using stiff bundles of reeds pushed into the marsh bed. The reed house is then built on top. In Peru in South America, some lake dwellers also live in houses made of reeds. They are built on huge, floating reed-rafts.

Structures

WHAT YOU NEED

scissors

card and corrugated card

pencil

glue

glitter

paints and brush

1 Paint a watery scene on a piece of card and decorate with glitter.

2 On another piece of card draw the outlines of small, medium and large buildings. Paint and cut them out.

3 Cut out small squares of thick card and glue to the backs of the buildings. Glue these onto the watery background scene to give a three dimensional effect.

What other structures over water can you make?

4 Draw a variety of arched bridges. Cut out and glue onto the picture, using the technique in step 3 to create a three dimensional effect.

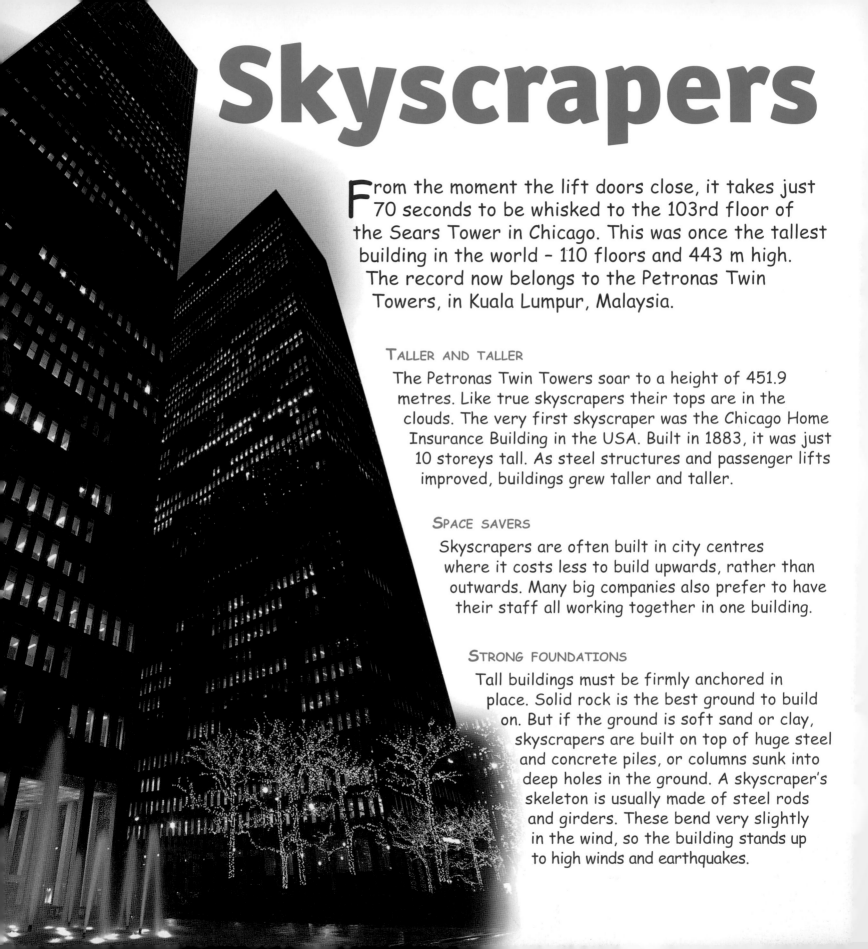

Skyscrapers

From the moment the lift doors close, it takes just 70 seconds to be whisked to the 103rd floor of the Sears Tower in Chicago. This was once the tallest building in the world – 110 floors and 443 m high. The record now belongs to the Petronas Twin Towers, in Kuala Lumpur, Malaysia.

TALLER AND TALLER

The Petronas Twin Towers soar to a height of 451.9 metres. Like true skyscrapers their tops are in the clouds. The very first skyscraper was the Chicago Home Insurance Building in the USA. Built in 1883, it was just 10 storeys tall. As steel structures and passenger lifts improved, buildings grew taller and taller.

SPACE SAVERS

Skyscrapers are often built in city centres where it costs less to build upwards, rather than outwards. Many big companies also prefer to have their staff all working together in one building.

STRONG FOUNDATIONS

Tall buildings must be firmly anchored in place. Solid rock is the best ground to build on. But if the ground is soft sand or clay, skyscrapers are built on top of huge steel and concrete piles, or columns sunk into deep holes in the ground. A skyscraper's skeleton is usually made of steel rods and girders. These bend very slightly in the wind, so the building stands up to high winds and earthquakes.

Structures

Fantasy metropolis

Using the same materials, what other tall buildings can you make?

WHAT YOU NEED

- variety of boxes
- box lid
- metallic paper and card
- foil
- long cardboard tube
- tape
- bottle top
- sequins
- stick
- glitter
- glue
- card
- coloured acetate

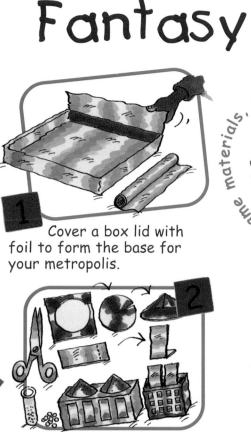

1 Cover a box lid with foil to form the base for your metropolis.

2 Cover boxes in a variety of shiny papers, foil and coloured acetate to make the buildings. Add small squares of foil or strips of holographic stickers and sequins to make windows.

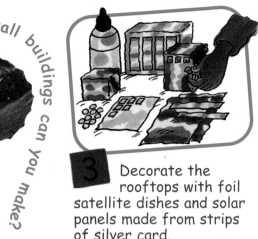

3 Decorate the rooftops with foil satellite dishes and solar panels made from strips of silver card.

4 Make a tall tower by wrapping foil around the long tube and decorating it with sequins.

Add a big satellite dish to the tower, made from a cone of foil taped to a stick. Put a foil-covered bottle top at the centre.

Crumbling columns

The ruins of the sanctuary of Athena at Delphi, Greece.

All over the world you can find the ruins of ancient buildings. Towering columns that were once part of a magnificent Greek temple stand alone among the crumbling ancient stones of another time. These weathered, ancient structures tell us a story of how people lived thousands of years ago, of how they built their cities, palaces and places of worship.

ANCIENT JIGSAW

Archaeologists study the remains of past human cultures. When a site is found, these scientists dig, or excavate, carefully among the ruins for buried objects. It takes hours and hours of work, but gradually the archaeologists can piece together information about ancient times. Every object found, whether it is a piece of pottery or stones from an archway or temple, helps to build up a picture of the culture of the time.

SUPPORTS AND FRAMEWORKS

The ancient Greeks built splendid temples. They tried to achieve beauty, symmetry, or balance in their buildings. The tall columns of a Greek temple surrounded a long, inner chamber. The columns gave the building its basic shape and design. Very thick walls were not needed. By evenly spacing the columns and placing them in rows, the building and roof were easily supported. Elaborate stone carvings added to the overall magnificence of the building. In ancient times, constructing a building was a very hard and lengthy process. Stone had to be carried long distances and carved by hand.

Structures

Greek ruins

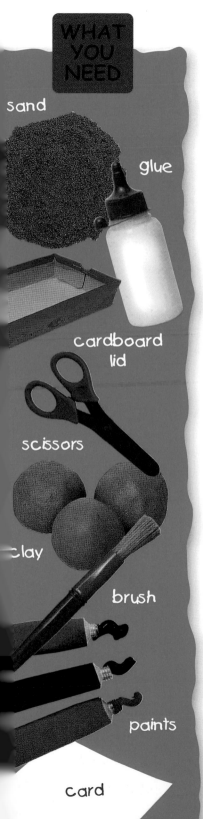

sand

glue

cardboard
lid

scissors

clay

brush

paints

card

1 Soften the clay and mould it into columns, a triangular arch, and bricks for loose rubble. Use the edge of the scissors to scratch textures onto the columns.

2 Glue sand onto the top and sides of a cardboard box lid, to make the base.

3 To make steps, cut a length of cardboard and fold it into a concertina. Paint, or glue on sand, then stick the steps to one of the long edges of the base.

Make clay pots and statues to add to your ruins

Paint your clay pillars, arch and bricks. Glue your arrangement into place on the base.

Standing stones

Buried in the rainforests of Mexico and standing tall on Easter Island in the Pacific Ocean, are mysterious, gigantic stone heads. They were made thousands of years ago by ancient peoples. And in many parts of Western Europe, ancient circles of stones can be found. The most famous of these is Stonehenge in southern Britain. But who built these strange stone monuments, and why?

GIANT HEADS

These giant carved heads on Easter Island were made about 1,000 to 400 years ago. They vary in height from 3-12 metres and some weigh more than 50 tonnes. They were carved from the soft, volcanic stone on the island, and lifted into place using ropes, wooden levers and piles of stones for support. The statues are probably of important people who became gods after they died. Other discoveries include stone statues of jaguars and snakes in Mexico, the only remaining evidence of the Olmec people, who lived 2,000 to 3,000 years ago.

The giant carved statues on Easter Island.

SUN TEMPLE?

The circle of huge standing stones known as Stonehenge was built over 4,000 years ago in southern England. But we can only guess how the stones were carried, cut into shape and placed upright. It is possible that Stonehenge was a temple to the Sun or an observatory - a place for keeping track of the movements of the Sun, Moon and stars. What we know for certain is that the stones are even older than the pyramids of Egypt.

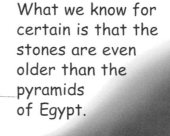

Structures

Totem pole

23

WHAT YOU NEED

clay

varnish

wire

brush

paints

1 Soften the clay and make several different shaped heads and one pair of feet with it.

2 Thread each shape onto a piece of wire to join them together. Make sure the feet are at the bottom.

3 When the clay is dry, paint your totem pole in bright colours, and varnish it.

Make a collection of totem poles with different shaped, brightly-coloured heads

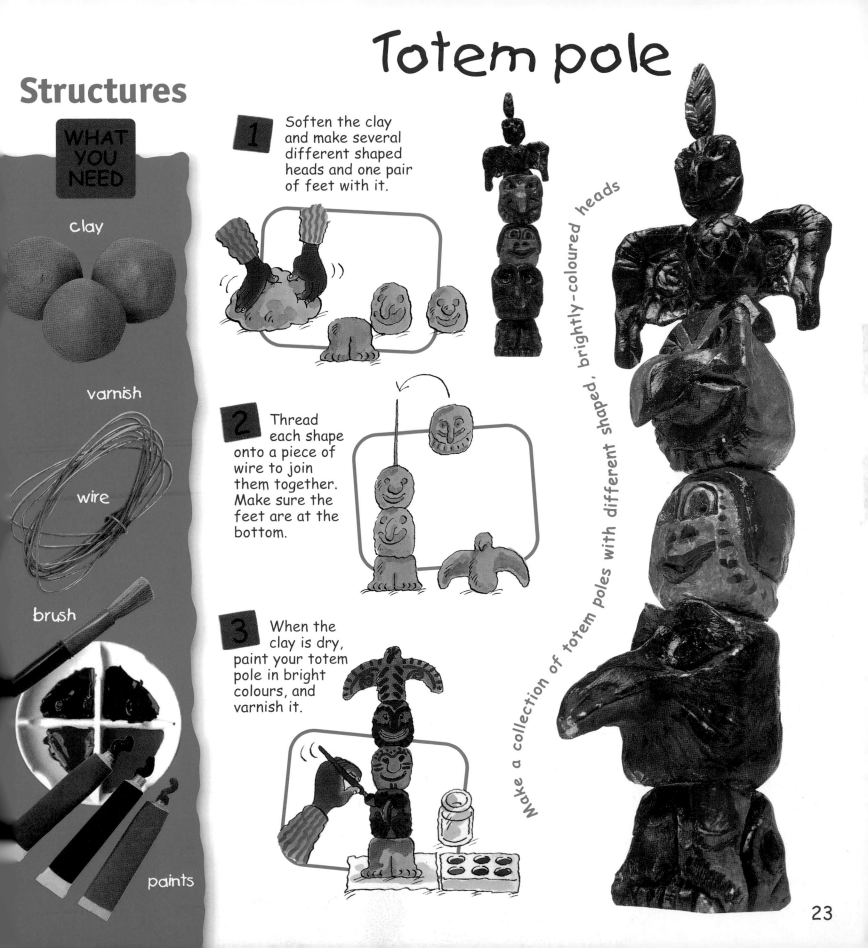

Mighty pyramids

Can you imagine building a pyramid with over two million stone blocks, each weighing more than two tonnes? The Great Pyramid at Giza in Egypt is this big. It was built about 4,500 years ago, as a tomb for Pharaoh Khufu. To guard against tomb robbers, the pharaoh's mummified body was laid in a secret chamber in the middle of the pyramid. Piled in the chamber were treasures for the king to use in the afterlife.

MUSCLE POWER

It took 20 years to build the pyramid at Giza. In Ancient Egypt, the only building tools were simple ones - copper chisels and saws, stone hammers and wooden set-squares. Instead of machine power, the Egyptians used the muscle power of hundreds of thousands of workers. They cut huge blocks of stone from nearby quarries and pulled them across the sand on rollers or sledges.

SAND AND RAMPS

The pyramid's base was a perfect square, marked out with string and pegs. As it grew higher, great slopes of sand were heaped up at the sides. The stones were pulled up these sand ramps and workers may have used levers to move the stones into their final positions. When the last block was in place, thousands of tonnes of sand had to be cleared away. This sand is still piled around the pyramid today. To finish it off, the pyramid was covered with dazzling white limestone, to make it shine in the sun. No one is sure why the pyramids were triangle-shaped. It may have been to give the pharaoh a stairway to the afterlife.

Pharaoh's tomb

Structures

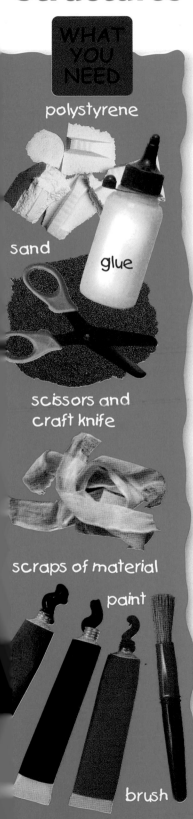

WHAT YOU NEED

polystyrene

sand

glue

scissors and craft knife

scraps of material

paint

brush

1 Draw a square and four equal triangles on the polystyrene.

With the scissors, mark brick shapes onto the four triangles.

3 Mix sand into the paint and cover the pyramid pieces. Glue 3 triangles to the square base.

4 Cut a long strip of polystyrene and mark steps on it with the scissors. Paint and glue to the fourth triangle. Make a small square hole at the top of this triangle, and attach to the model.

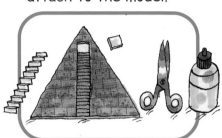

5 Cut out a cat god and a tomb from the polystyrene and paint. Use the material to make a mummy. Paint a square of polystyrene with hieroglyphics.

Make some treasure out of beads and buttons to put in your pharaoh's tomb

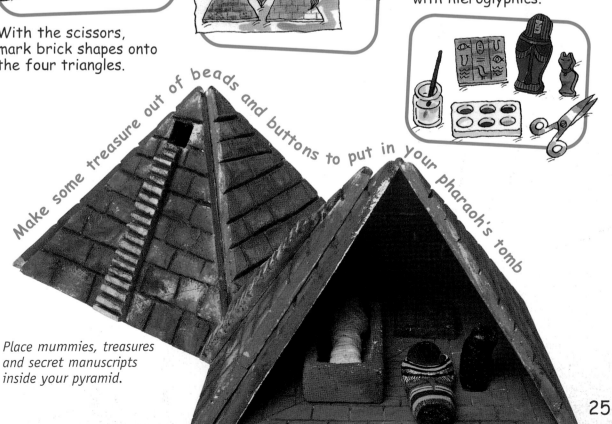

Place mummies, treasures and secret manuscripts inside your pyramid.

25

Floor art

Tough and colourful

The first mosaics were made of tiny pebbles. Since mosaics were used mainly for floors and pavements, the materials had to be strong enough for people to walk on. Marble or limestone were often used because they could be cut into small pieces and came in a range of colours. Stone is used in mosaics today, as well as glass, gold, silver, semi-precious stones and ceramic tile pieces.

Precious stones

The ancient Mayans and Aztecs of Mexico made beautiful mosaics from semi-precious stones. Turquoise was their favourite material, but they also used garnet, quartz, beryl, malachite, jadeite and gold. The mosaics decorated all sorts of items, including masks, shields and helmets.

Imagine doing a jigsaw puzzle with over 100,000 pieces! Mosaics are like jigsaw puzzles. They are pictures made from thousands of tiny coloured pieces. The pieces are small squares, triangles or other shapes that fit closely together to make a regular pattern. The ancient Romans decorated their floors, fountains, walls and baths with beautiful mosaics.

Roman scenes

Roman mosaics showed gods and many kinds of scenes bordered with geometric patterns.
The floor of an average room in a Roman house needed over 100,000 mosaic pieces! To make a mosaic, two or three layers of mortar, a kind of cement, were spread on a thick stone base.
A sketch of the overall picture was drawn on to this and the mosaic pieces pressed into place.

Structures

Mosaic

1 Draw the outline of a picture in pencil.

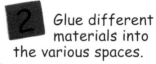

2 Glue different materials into the various spaces.

3 Mount your mosaic picture.

Make a gallery of mosaics for your bedroom wall

Turrets and ramparts

Most castles were built in the Middle Ages by important people, such as lords or kings and queens. As well as being splendid homes, the castles were also powerful fortresses. With their strong walls and high towers, they were designed to keep out enemies. Most castles were built on a hill and surrounded by a moat. When the drawbridge over the moat was pulled up, the castle became an island stronghold.

THE GATEHOUSE

The weakest part of a castle was the entrance. This was protected by a tall gatehouse full of soldiers, thick doors, and perhaps an iron gate, called a portcullis. The portcullis guarded the entrance, and was pulled up and down by winding equipment in the gatehouse.

WALLS AND BATTLEMENTS

The battlements at the top of the castle walls had gaps for soldiers in the castle to fire through. Narrow slits in the walls were perfect for firing arrows out, but too narrow to let enemy fire come in. Many castles also had stone parapets jutting out from the tops of the walls. Soldiers could drop heavy stones or boiling water on top of attackers through holes in the parapets.

ENEMY ATTACK!

Soldiers on the battlements had to keep a look out for enemy soldiers climbing up over the battlements using long ladders, or tall, wooden towers on wheels. To fight their way inside a castle, soldiers used giant catapults to hurl stone boulders at the walls. Large crossbows on wheels fired huge heavy bolts, and battering rams were swung from chains, or rolled on wheels to smash down walls and doors.

Structures

Castle stronghold

1 Cut slit windows and turrets from two pieces of card as shown. Roll the card into tubes and glue to make two towers.

2 As shown, cut out 3 more lengths of card to make the walls and entrance. Stick them to the towers to make the main structure of the castle.

3 Stick lolly sticks together to make the drawbridge. Paint and glue them to the piece of card that was cut out from the door entrance. Paint the castle.

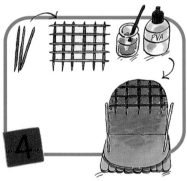

4 Glue cocktail sticks together into a grid to make a gate. Paint and glue to the inner door. Make holes, and thread string through the drawbridge and entrance wall so that your drawbridge can open and close.

5 Glue scrunched-up newspaper to a large piece of card to make grass banks around a moat and a middle mound for the castle to sit on. Paint, and cover the moat with blue tissue paper.

Make flags to stick on the turrets

Rooftops

Roofs are like umbrellas. They cover the tops of buildings, protecting them from the weather. Rain and snow easily slide off sloping roofs. You see sloping roofs in countries where the weather is wet. In places where there is very little rain, the buildings usually have flat roofs.

PAGODA CURVES

Other roof shapes include tall, thin church spires, domes, and the tiered roofs on pagodas. Pagodas are a type of tower, with many storeys, or tiers. Each tier has a decorated, overhanging roof that curves up at the edges. Many pagodas are places of worship, such as Buddhist temples.

STRAW, TAR AND TILES

The first roofs were probably made of straw, leaves, branches or reeds. Thatched roofs like this are still used in some parts of the world. Flat roofs are usually covered with special roofing felt and tar. Sloping roofs have a timber, concrete or steel framework. This is covered in sheets of corrugated metal, or tiles made from clay or slate.

KEEPING WARM

Roofs are often lined with a layer of material, called insulation, which has lots of air pockets. Since air traps heat, the insulation helps to keep a building warm in winter and cool in summer.

The layered roofs on this tall pagoda protect it from the sunshine and the rain.

High-rise gardens

Structures

1 Cut windows and doors from the cardboard boxes to make your basic house structures.

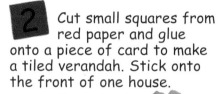

2 Cut small squares from red paper and glue onto a piece of card to make a tiled verandah. Stick onto the front of one house.

3 Paint your houses in bright colours.

Paint bottle tops to make flower pots for your roof garden too

4 Fold a narrow length of card into a concertina shape. Glue onto one side of a house to make a staircase.

5 Make grass blades from green card, and flowers by glueing lengths of string with sequins on top.

6 Cut small card heads and glue to cocktail sticks to make people. Use tissue paper for their clothes.

31

Golden domes

All over the world, domes decorate the tops of important and beautiful buildings. The ancient Romans used them on temples such as the Pantheon in Rome. You can also see them on cathedrals, mosques and Muslim tombs. Look for domes on top of more ordinary buildings, too, such as museums and even large shops. Some domes are left plain, but many are shining gold, brightly coloured, or even covered with richly patterned tiles.

WORLD FAMOUS

The Mosque of Omar, in Jerusalem, is also called the Dome of the Rock because of its magnificent, dome-shaped golden roof. The Taj Mahal in India, Florence Cathedral in Italy, and St Basil's Cathedral in Moscow are other world-famous domed buildings.

GIANT SPACES

Domed structures are difficult to build, but they create huge spaces inside buildings. Domes are built from triangular or many-sided pieces which spread out the weight of the structure. Geodesic domes are strong, lightweight, modern domes used for factories, sports stadiums, theatres or exhibitions. They can be made of materials as different as plastic or cardboard.

The spectacular domes of Ubadiah mosque in Kuala Kangsar, Malaysia.

Structures

WHAT YOU NEED

paper

coloured mounting card

pencil

gold, siver and metallic colour paper

pastels

glue

Glittering and shiny domes glistening in the moonlight

1 Draw an outline of a domescape.

2 Use the pastels and metallic papers to colour and form patterned domes.

3 Mount your picture.

33

Building bridges

The best way to cross a river, canyon or other kind of obstacle is to use a bridge. A bridge saves you having to swim, go by boat, or travel a long way around the obstacle. A bridge can be a simple tree trunk laid across the gap, or a massive suspension bridge that stretches hundreds of metres in front of you.

WEIGHT CARRIERS

A bridge must be able to carry its own weight and the weight of all the traffic crossing it. A beam bridge is the simplest kind of bridge, such as a plank across a stream. Each end is supported by the bank. But beam bridges are only good for bridging a short distance. Arch bridges have a series of arches which carry the weight outwards along two curving paths down to the ground. The Sydney Harbour Bridge in Australia is an arch bridge. Made of steel, it has a span of nearly 503 metres.

The Golden Gate Bridge, San Francisco, USA.

SUSPENSION BRIDGES

A suspension bridge is a modern version of the simple rope bridge used by people for thousands of years. Most of the world's really large bridges, such as the Golden Gate bridge in San Francisco, are suspension bridges. The bridge hangs, or is suspended, from thick steel cables strung between tall towers at each end. The ends of the cables are anchored firmly on either side of the bridge. The cables carry the weight of the bridge and its traffic to the towers and then to the ground. The towers must be very strong and fixed firmly in the ground. The Golden Gate stretches out for 1,280 metres.

Structures

Swingbridge canyon

WHAT YOU NEED

buttons

sand

card

string

newspaper

sponge

matchbox

lolly sticks

scissors

glue

paints and brush

1 Scrunch up newspaper and glue it down on a large piece of card to make a canyon with a river running through the middle of it.

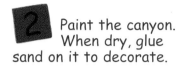

2 Paint the canyon. When dry, glue sand on it to decorate.

3 Glue lollysticks onto two lengths of string to form swing bridges. Stick the bridges over the river.

4 Cut pieces of sponge into bush and tree shapes. Paint and stick onto your canyon model.

Make model cars from matchboxes. Use buttons and circles of card as the wheels. Paint and decorate.

What other materials can you use to make bridges?

Ribbons of black

Roads join villages, towns and cities across all the countries of the world. They allow goods and people to be carried quickly and easily from place to place. Some roads are just dirt tracks wide enough for a single car. Others are huge motorways with many lanes and trucks, coaches and cars zooming at high speeds along them. In cities, spaghetti junctions like the one in the picture above form a tangle of busy roads crossing above, below and around each other. Many people think roadbuilding harms the environment and should be stopped.

MOVING EARTH

New roads are often built across open countryside. The roadbuilders must find out what kind of soil and rock an area is made of. They must also look at how much damage an area will suffer, and work out the cost of the road. The route is then marked out, ready for the huge, earth-moving machines.

MAKING LINKS

The Romans built long straight roads, linking towns and cities in their empire, and enabling Roman troops to march quickly from place to place. The world's longest road joins Texas in the USA with Valparaiso in Chile. It is over 26,000 kilometres long!

Structures

Cardboard junction

1 Draw an outline of a road on a large piece of card.

2 Scrunch up newspaper and glue onto the card to make high grass verges. Paint your model.

3 Cut both ends off a plastic bottle and stick it onto any part of the road.

4 Cut out and paint a length of corrugated card and glue over the top of the bottle to make a flyover.

5 Draw, paint and cut out road signs and trees. Stick each one on the end of a cocktail stick and use small pieces of clay as stands.

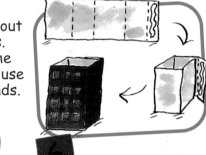

6 Add cardboard buildings, zebra crossings etc. to your road scene. Use model cars to drive on the winding roads.

Play a game of cars with your friends on your winding road model

Beacons of light

Sailing a ship close to shore at night has always been dangerous. There are often rocks, sandbanks, reefs, cliffs or other unseen hazards. To help navigators steer their way safely, guiding lights warn of the dangers ahead. The sweeping beam from a lighthouse beacon illuminates the night sky and the dark shore waters, guiding ships safely around the hidden dangers.

TOWERS OF LIGHT

Most lighthouses are simple towers made of brick, stone, wood or metal. They are built on coastlines, peninsulas, on rocks, in the sea itself, and at ports and harbours. Some lighthouses are solid towers. Others have a platform with a house-like structure on top. And some are no more than a metal frame with a light on top.

FLASHES IN THE DARK

In ancient times, lighthouses were lit up with fire. Later, oil lamps were used. Today, lighthouses have a bright electric light and a special lens that revolves around the light, making it blink. Each lighthouse has its own special pattern of blinking light called a characteristic.

Structures

WHAT YOU NEED

paints and brush

shells and pebbles

silver paper

card

scissors

cocktail sticks

yellow tissue paper

glue

glitter

string

clay

1

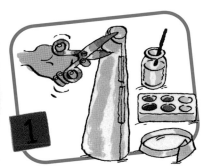

Roll a piece of card into a slim cone shape. Cut off the top and bottom so the cone stands up. Cut out round windows and paint.

2

Soften the clay and make a rocky base around the lighthouse with a shallow dip in it for your soap to go in. Decorate with shells and pebbles.

3

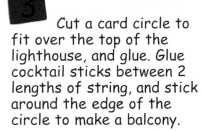

Cut a card circle to fit over the top of the lighthouse, and glue. Glue cocktail sticks between 2 lengths of string, and stick around the edge of the circle to make a balcony.

4

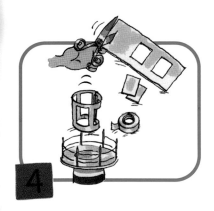

Cut square holes in a length of card. Stick the 2 ends together to make a circular tower which will fit inside the balcony.

Get a scented soap for your novelty dish!

5

Make a cone from card, and paint. Place on top of the tower. Scrunch silver foil and yellow tissue paper into a ball. Add glitter. Place inside the tower as a shining beacon.

Glass-blowing

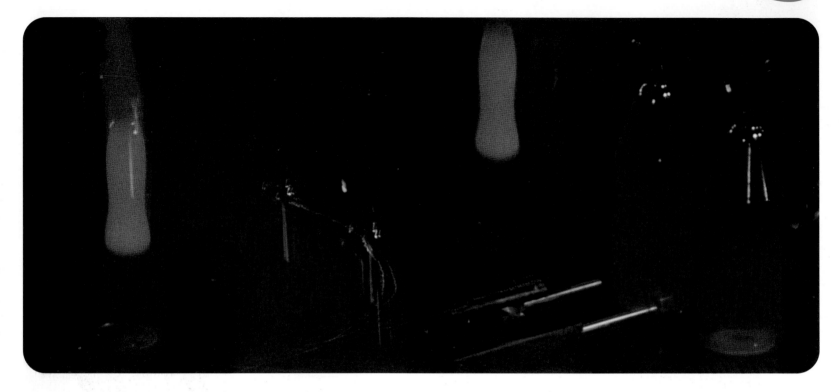

What does the word glass make you think of? Something to drink from? The material windows are made of? We use glass to make thousands of different objects. It is one of the most useful materials in the world and also one of the most beautiful.

MELTED SAND

Glass was invented by the ancient Egyptians. They first made it about 5,000 years ago by melting a mixture of sand, lime, soda and other materials. They used the glass for making beads. The first glass containers were made about 4,000 years ago, by pouring liquid glass around a clay mould.

BLOWN SHAPES

About 2,000 years ago, a way of shaping glass by blowing air into it was invented. It was like blowing air into a balloon. Today, some beautiful and expensive glass vases, bowls and ornaments are still made like this. But most modern glass is made by machines. Sand, soda ash and limestone are heated in a furnace to a temperature of 1,500°C. The liquid glass is cooled into a thin, sticky material and then moulded into shape or flattened into sheets.

FLATTENING AND COLOURING

Window glass is made by flattening molten glass between rollers into flat, smooth sheets. To make coloured glass, different chemicals are added to the mixture while it is being made.

Materials

WHAT YOU NEED

glass tumblers

grout

bowl of water

glass beads

palette knife
or spatula

Make a set of colourful beaded glasses to give as a present

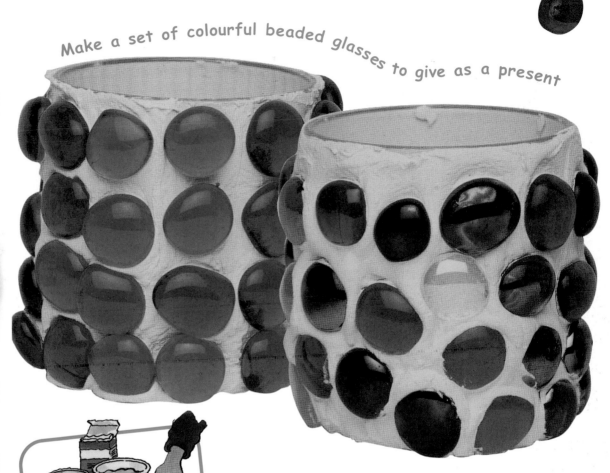

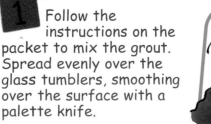

1 Follow the instructions on the packet to mix the grout. Spread evenly over the glass tumblers, smoothing over the surface with a palette knife.

2 Press glass beads into the grout. You can make different patterns with the coloured beads.

3 Leave to dry.

You can use your decorated tumblers as pencil holders.

Useful plastics

COLOURED CHEMICALS

Plastics are artificial materials that can be shaped into almost any form. Most plastics are made from chemicals found in oil. The oil is turned into plastic granules, or pellets in a chemical factory. Dyes are often mixed with the granules to colour them. Some different types of plastic include acrylic, nylon, polystyrene, celluloid, PVC, and polythene.

FANTASTIC PLASTIC

Plastics are very useful materials because they do not rot, rust, or carry electricity. They are also waterproof and lightweight. Plastics are used to make parts for cars, aeroplanes and buildings. Plastic nylon fibres are used to make clothes. Shatter-proof plastic bottles and jars have replaced glass ones. And bright, soft plastic toys are sturdy and safe enough for babies to play with.

Toys and toothbrushes, bottles and buckets, packaging and pipes... all sorts of things are made of plastics. They can be any colour of the rainbow, or totally see-through. Some plastics are hard and stiff, but others are rubbery. They can bend and stretch without cracking.

MOULDING AND SHAPING

First, the plastic is heated until it is soft and runny. Then it is poured into a mould and left to cool. To make it into sheets, the liquid plastic is flattened between heavy rollers.

Robot dog

Materials

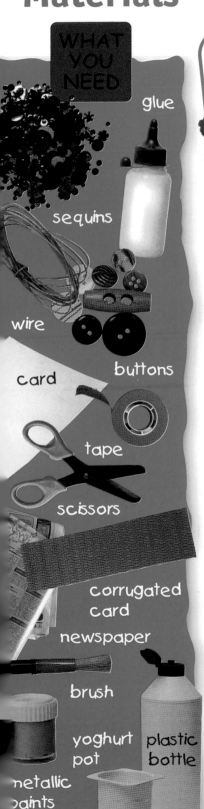

glue

sequins

wire

card

buttons

tape

scissors

corrugated card

newspaper

brush

yoghurt pot

plastic bottle

metallic paints

1 Roll card into tubes to make legs. Glue them to one side of the bottle.

2 Cut the top edge off a yoghurt pot and glue onto the end of the bottle to make the dog's face.

3 Rip up pieces of newspaper and glue all over the bottle and legs.

4 Paint the legs, body and face of your dog, with a metallic colour.

5 Cut out ears and a tail as shown. Paint and tape them onto the body. Make wire whiskers.

Make other plastic robot animals such as a cat or a mouse

Stick on buttons and sequins for the eyes, and for decoration on the body.

43

Future homes

What will homes be like in the future? Will we live in underwater cities, under the ground or even in space? Anything is possible. At the start of the 20th century, there were no jet planes, TVs or computers. Now, we can't imagine life without them. So we can only guess at the changes to come.

Eco-homes

The number of people in the world is growing all the time. For this reason, future homes need to cause less pollution and save and use energy more wisely. Some houses have already been built to do this. They have solar panels on the roof to trap and make electricity from sunlight. Insulation material keeps the heat in, or out, so less heating or air-conditioning is needed. And rainwater drains from the roof into tanks to supply water.

Mission to mars

Scientists are already planning to build camps on Mars. These will allow astronauts to explore the planet properly on a future mission. An unmanned ERV, or Earth Return Vehicle will land first. It will then prepare for the arrival of the astronauts two years later. Because Mars is similar to Earth, oxygen and water could be produced on the planet. This means less equipment and fewer supplies will need to be brought from Earth.

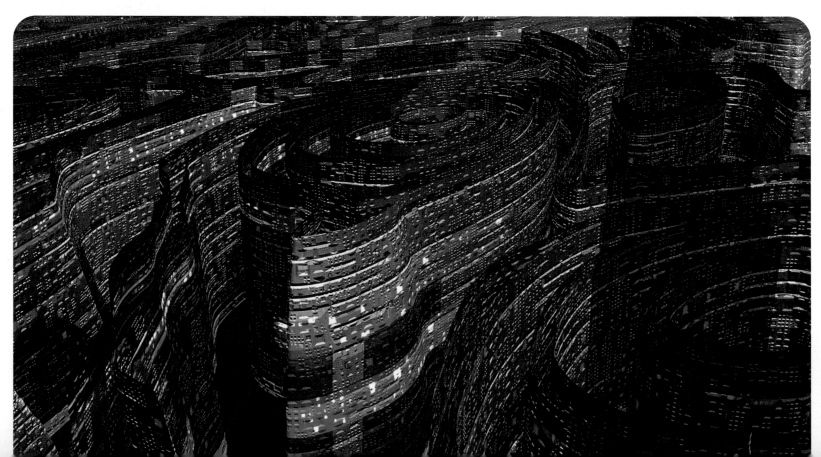

Futuristic city

Structures

WHAT YOU NEED

tape

glue

polystyrene

wire

matchboxes

pencil

buttons

bubble wrap

foil

sequins

foil cake cups

cardboard

scissors

paintbrush

plastic bottles and containers

lver paint

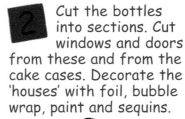

2 Cut the bottles into sections. Cut windows and doors from these and from the cake cases. Decorate the 'houses' with foil, bubble wrap, paint and sequins.

1 Draw three circles of different sizes on card and cut out. Cover with foil and paint.

Attach astronauts to wire and make them float above the circular platforms.

3 Take 3 containers of different depths. Glue one onto each of the 3 circles, and stick to the base, overlapping to make platforms at different levels, as shown.

4 Stick the bottle space homes onto the platforms.

5 Make space cars by painting matchboxes and glueing on buttons for wheels. Stick on a curve of bubble wrap for the roof.

45

Glossary and Index